AF414487

A Moment With Two Dreamers

Kim-Linh Vo

A Moment With Two Dreamers © 2023
Kim-Linh Vo

All rights reserved.

No part of this publication may be reproduced, stored in a retrieval system, or transmitted, in any form or by any means, electronic, mechanical, photocopying, recording or otherwise, without the prior written permission of the presenters.

Kim-Linh Vo asserts the moral right to be identified as the author of this work.

Presentation by *BookLeaf Publishing*

Web: www.bookleafpub.com

E-mail: info@bookleafpub.com

ISBN: 9789358310054

First edition 2023

ACKNOWLEDGEMENT

First, I'd like to acknowledge you, the person who picked up this book and shared this journey through my poetry with me. Without you, this would just be a dust collector or a shelf decoration, so I am endlessly grateful to you.

A million thanks go to everyone who supported me while I wrote these poems.

My older sisters, Kim-Anh and Kim-Tien, took my cover photo and helped me decipher what I wanted the cover to look like on top of being free, around-the-clock editors. My younger sister, Kim-Minh, made really good food and took a lot of things off my plate so I could focus, and here is the mandatory shout-out to Minh-Long, who is the funniest and coolest bro in the world. Thank you so much to my mom for encouraging me and raising me with enough creativity and discipline to complete this challenge in the first place, and my dad, whose late-night talks over ramen and advice tidbits on car rides inspired the poem "Five Thousand Years In A Jade Bracelet." I definitely can't thank either of them enough for their support though.

Special thanks also go to my best friend Juan, who (despite all the times I wanted to stop the challenge) cheered me on, hyped me up, got on my case about not writing a poem regularly, and was usually the first person to read and give me feedback on my poems, even though poetry really isn't his thing. Thanks to Neil, who also kept up with my writing process and reviewed my work, even if it was at an absurdly late time. Thanks to my teachers: Mr. Jones (who first fostered my creative writing hobby), Ms. Rossi (who always had new perspectives that helped me develop my style), and Mr. Nakamura (who entertained so many of my questions with genuine answers no matter how weird they were and first suggested I find a way to publish a small collection of poetry). Finally, a huge thank you to Mrs. Harb, who edited some of my poems and gave me great insights while on summer break and overseas. Thank you so much!

A Moment with Two Dreamers

Sit with me for a moment in this maniacal universe of ours.
Amber skies fall over us, and for this stolen moment,
all is
quiet.

The hum of the universe sings for you and me;
my feet brush drying grass from my splintering swing.
I reach for the universe with you by my side,
hoping, pleading someone will understand:

These are the words I fear to speak,
polished and pared down so they reach you
like the first snow settles on your sleepy eyes —
If this is the last you see of me, I will be glad to have met
you.

In this moment, I shout to the world with my soundless
words,
do they reach you?

Where The Poets Bleed

2

Take me to the place where the poets bleed,
and each carmine drop turns into dulcet tones that sing
the symphonies their voices cannot.

Let me run wild in the fields where the romantics sigh;
they see the world in a blushing phosphorescence
and send us chasing rosy sunrises across the horizon.

Or drown me in the lakes where the mourners lament,
and the tear-stained pages of their requiems
sink with the weight of the grief woven into their words.

Take me far away from where the rest of us wander,
where the rest of us go to
die.

The Path of Paper Wings

We stumble out to the city lights like moths to a flame.
A cyclic pursuit of a promised sanctuary,
trodden with the steps of the thousands before us,
we cling to the hope of an eternal sunrise,
a haven where we could let our bruised bodies rest,
a hearth where we could let our iron swords rust.

We followed the golden path to the end,
wrapped ourselves in those napalm lights.
We tasted heaven in feathers shoved down our throats;
the city was never as blinding as it was then.

Did you feel it, too? The phantom
chills waltzing down your spine,
the echo of ancient voices in the dark,
silver flames kindling somewhere
inside your heart reaching for
more, always more…

If only we realized before the promise of safety exhausted
our paper wings:
comfort could never satiate any burning
soul.

Champagne Lights

We haven't had a taste of the sun
since you decided it was yours.
We've forgotten what its warmth was
since you locked us away inside.
Glimmers of hope peeked through the windows,
but sooner or later,
you always remember to draw the blinds.

Like laces on corsets or keys for bird cages,
it seems we let you force us into submission. You gave us
no choice other than
to pose with sealed lips
and hold your arm while we smile politely.

But we've found a way out of the box
to a paradise of forbidden pleasure.
Here we can dance and sing and tap and twirl.
Here, in the dark of night, we are free to be real.
Here, we can let our souls run wild.
We have found our own sun
in the glow of champagne lights.

The Lady of the Unnamed Kingdom

They say even the gods envied her beauty,
and dreams rushed to her bedside to guard her sleep.
They say the beast was captivated by the sleeping princess,
and his calamitous love was the only thing he could
surrender.
They say he took her from the spire one night;
the torn hem of her dress was the last anyone saw of her,
but they say his love for her goodness made her into a god.

Lady of the Unnamed Kingdom,
did the same faithless town that sang your praises
not leave you on a cliff at the will of their gods?
Where is the weakness in your love
if not their rose-covered envy?

The perils in the river and Death's door greeted you;
it was at the sight of your love, not his, that they turned you
away.
(the town rejoiced when you joined their altars,
they can no longer tell your story)

To Make A Poet From A Politician

What would it take to make a poet of a politician?
I suppose their knees would protrude from our classroom desks,
but they could get used to the awkward position.

We would need all the best teachers,
so we'll send an emergency call throughout the nation,
search high and low for a teacher with all the prowess of
Neruda or Winston
(and of course we'd give them quite the promotion).

They might divide themselves into their cliques
and sit on opposite sides of the classroom.
That'd be just like a regular high schooler,
so they'd fit right in with all their posing costumes.

They wouldn't be used to doing assignments so fast;
let's start with something much closer to their pace,
and send them home with practice annotations,
highlighters, and extra copies (just in case).

The change of scene would make them students, not poets.
They may be able to wrap their speeches in silk
but no teacher, metaphor, or assignment could infuse their
words with gold —
this is no land of honey or milk.

The Second Waltz

I sit at the piano again,
my fingers, shaking, poised over keys.
She does not seem pleased today either.

Shostakovich, you must also be
disappointed. My chords are lifeless,
void, dense and bulky on ivory.

Black ink blurs, what am I doing here?
My fingers are moving too quickly,
they will exhaust themselves much too soon.

"Try again." She is trying her best.
It cannot be easy, steering her
ship alone. I do just as she says.

My song whimpers as if through water;
it drifts farther and farther away —
Is she saying something to me now?

"So much potential." I hear her sigh.
It hurts more than songs and splintering keys.
I must focus. Slow the pace and dance.

Five Thousand Years in a Jade Bracelet

I wore the five thousand years
in the jade bracelet around my wrists;
their roots sunk themselves into my arms.

Over midnight meals,
my father passed down their poetry,
 hoping I would make it my own.
He pointed out his scars, flying a world away
with stories behind each mark:
the men in tailored, tattered uniforms
stared in awe at his fruit,
the sun was bright on the hill
when he stole the soldiers' sugarcane,
the bombs rattled all the bones in his body
through the clay shelter his parents built.

In car rides home from school,
my mother drummed their lessons into me,
hoping to build a marvel from my faults.
She showed me how to sow buttons
on my polyester blouses,
like the ones she fastened into the silk dresses
 she left in the flames,
and how to recognize the best gold,
like her mother's wedding ring, that she
the one traded for rice in a strange city long ago.

My sister's bracelet hung on her wrist wherever she went;
mine sat in a jewelry box beneath my bed.
I slipped it on and off my fingers like a party trick,
forced every language on my tongue except for theirs,
ran away from the five thousand years that continue in my
blood.

Now I stand among the weeds of where they rest,
a stray child back on their parents' doorstep.
They slip the bracelet on my wrist,
and the roots grow into my skin again.

Moonchild

To the nights I spent wondering
where I fit into the tapestry of time,
To the song I heard in the hum
of a universe that never slept,
To the stars that showed me
a million paths to a million futures,
can you see me too?

To the pillows that collect my tears
over the words I cannot speak.
To the walls that listen to my ramblings
of a past I cannot reach,
To the journals that record my dreams
of crane wings and cherry blossom springs,
what stories could you tell?

To the world I turn away from
at the end of every day,
with its wounds I wish I could sew,
To the ones I only ever
leave with less
and their shoes I cannot fill,
will you wait a little longer?

So I'll stare up at the night again and again,
play the melodies of my universe on repeat,
walk the tightrope to its end
as I feel my way through darkness,

for I am but a
moonchild
in a sea of stars.

Chasing Rain and Forgotten Games

I remember staring at my mother's car window,
rooting for rain droplets in imaginary races.
I remember drawing people with triangles and boxes
and quarters of suns in page corners.
I remember hogging the best playground swing;
jumping from so high was the scariest thing back then.
And I remember the boy from math class
holding up his hand to tease me for my height.
I bet he has much more to worry about now.

Don't you ever miss the days
of weaving realms from clouds in the sky?
The subjects from our pretend kingdoms
must think we abandoned them long ago.
Would they mourn the loss of the stuffed animals
and superheroes that once covered our bed?
Would they raise their eyebrows
at our black closets and white-lie résumés?

I bet they wouldn't even recognize us for the child they
once knew.

Shadows of the Same Road

12

I walk the same street every day,
the same shadows in my wake.

What a bitter twist of fate:
to be stuck, still on this road.

I'm growing tired of my shadow
and its ever-present echoes;
I don't dare stop now
but one step ahead is all I can be.
Another day,
unchanged.

The Precipice

My journey started after dark;
I took the long way up.
I watched your ascent to the top
of the precipice,
bounding up the steps you left behind.
Your journey carved itself into the stones;
my finger traced each memory they told.

In my trance of wonder,
my eyes stuck to your mirage,
I stumbled barefoot along the path.
The rocks tore slits in my feet,
crimson regret pouring out of each cut,
but still, I clung to your shadows
as my own held on to
me.

You disappeared into the night,
leaving me nothing
but a thousand footsteps I could never fill.
Your memory was
my saving grace,
my last shred of hope,
my untimely undoing,

but I had never felt so weightless as I did when I fell.

Elegy to a Broken Soul

Where have you gone this time?
Your body draping over the windowsill,
your hair grazing your paling cheeks,
your runaway gaze must meet so many sights.

The moon looks lonely tonight, sitting among the stars —
your eyes must know the feeling.
I've come to hate that look in your eyes:
distant, fleeting,
close enough to keep me here,
far enough to see this dangerous game.

Please don't leave me here, don't you dare run.
Map your constellations from shrapnel you weave into my
skin,
chart your seas with my blood, arm yourself with my
bones.
I'd give them all to you if you could find your way back to
me.

How could you leave me here,
alone at your windowsill?
The moon is not so kind with a stranger.

Hellbent

It is just like you to lose yourself like this,
among the mirror shards at your feet,
drunk on their blind jealousy that drips down your lips.
Even Icarus would be humbled at the sight of you now.

Why do your wings still beg to touch the sky,
even as shimmering wax sears your downfall on your skin?
You bask in the adulation, the envy you provoke,
but as the story goes: "the higher you rise, the farther you
fall"

So when your tendrils suffocate your selfish pride,
I'll see you here at the bottom,
clinging to the hem of my torn, blood-soaked gown.
It is just like us to lose ourselves like this.

The Ramblings of a Sane Man

I come to this narrative with unequivocal certainty
that I am of a sound mind,
though there will undoubtedly be many people
who doubt the legitimacy of my story.
My exceptional sight must be the root of such doubts,
for I have myself a green glass door through which the
world presents itself to me,
and through which I met a man
identical to me in every manner but age.

Smooth as glazed porcelain and soft as a cotton swaddle,
his face was untouched by the trifles
of the road before him,
with the exception of a scar I knew well from my own face,
a scar that traced a path from the bottom of his eye to his
lips.
He told me his present
and recounted his troubles as a child would:
ripe with the clutch of naiveté and ignorance.
I concentrated on the syncopated rhythm
of water droplets behind me
as he sat on the cold tile and spun his tales.
All the while, I stifled a fit of incredulous laughter:
How could such a simple mind think anything of itself?

Another man, again identical to me in every manner but
age, greeted me.
He bore the same scar from his lip to his eye,
but it nearly hid itself in the wrinkles
rippling across his skin.
The man hobbled past virescent glass shards
scattered across blood-stained tile
to stare at me with sad eyes.
I asked him of my future,
of my glittering triumphs and glorious accolades.
He told me of a future so repugnant,
it could not have possibly been mine.
He must have been the maddest man in the universe.
    Indeed, the man maddest in the universe,
            to think that I would ever be less than

In the Face of Mortality

Perhaps it is not death we fear,
but our names being plucked from the air.

We fear the ones we care for most
clearing space in their minds
for the lives they will lead without us.

We fear the possibility of all the
rejections, December nights, and bitter sorrows
amounted to an empty legacy,
as if the alphabet blocks we've built
all collapse,
only to be left forgotten in closed drawers.

We fear the prospect
of what no storybook could tell,
what no human could comprehend,
what no myth could ever guess:
the unknown succeeding our very last breath.

It is not death we fear,
perhaps it is pain.

A Train to the End of the World

I took a train to the end of the world,
where they say Time stands still,
exhausted among the weeds.
The tracks stretched past
forgotten valleys and desolate horizons;
the farther the train carried us,
the further there was to go.

The passengers saw their futures playing in pieces
through misty windows, an enigmatic haze
of what-could-be's.
The train rattled on, weaving stories and dreams,
each compartment a world, a microcosm of desires.

But the most captivating sight was not what we would see,
it was what we would miss,
the moments that would slip through our fingers
like sand in a sieve.

I never reached the end of the world —
I can't say if the train ever did either.
I remain where I left off:
among the weeds and dreams of all the places I'll never
reach.

The Hero's 1001th Face

My pencil and cursor must both be impatient
from waiting on me to draw
these polished words from my throat.
"Creation is a wonderful thing."
I wonder how many ways can I rewrite my emotions,
capturing each one in glass jars of similes and stories,
between the lines of alliteration and rhyme.
How many ways can I dissect my brain
to breathe life into symbols?
"Creation is a messy thing."
I force meaning into
the droplets of rain in play races I traced down the car
window of my mother's car,
or the day-old tea on the windowsill,
or my favorite cautionary tales from long-dead
civilizations.
It appears my ink has run dry.
"Creation is a taxing thing."
And yet, my fingers itch to draw the hero's 1001th face.
His eyes begin to take shape on the page,
    then a pointed nose and a smirking lip.
        Next, a quaffed updo? Delicate waves? Unruly curls?
            The last line is drawn and off he goes,
            running and running from the ordinary world
I can reach him, trap his story
back on his page in my glass jars
if only I keep his idea in my sight.
It seems my fingers give me no choice,
creation is a human thing.

www.ingramcontent.com/pod-product-compliance
Lightning Source LLC
Chambersburg PA
CBHW070734160726
48003CB00006BA/2506